Animals Adapt

by Lian Wu

PEARSON

Glenview, Illinois • Boston, Massachusetts • Chandler, Arizona
Upper Saddle River, New Jersey

Animals adapt. The ways they look and act change over time. These changes help them to solve problems.

Why do animals adapt? Animals adapt to stay alive.

Lions adapted. They have strong teeth. This helps lions eat zebras.

Zebras adapted too. They have strong legs. They can run away from lions.

Fish Adapt

Fish cannot live on land. They adapted to live underwater. Fish have scales, fins, and gills.

Fish swim underwater.

Fins help fish to swim. Gills help fish take in air.

Fish do not have skin. Fish have scales. Scales protect the fish from the water.

Beavers Adapt

Beavers live in rivers or lakes. They have fur to stay warm. Their wide tails help them swim. Beavers have strong teeth. The teeth help them eat trees.

A beaver builds a home.

Beavers build homes in the water. They use branches and leaves. A beaver goes into its home under the water.

Turtles Adapt

Turtles can walk on land. They are slow. Turtles have hard shells. They can hide inside.

A turtle comes up for air.

Turtles can swim underwater. But they cannot take in air underwater. Turtles do not need air often.

Rabbits Adapt

Rabbits are small. They adapted to stay safe. Long ears help rabbits hear other animals.

Rabbits have strong legs. They can get away from other animals. Many animals cannot catch rabbits.

Think about animals you see. Think about where they live.

How did these animals adapt?